FIRST SOLOS

for the
HORN
PLAYER

TRANSCRIBED AND ARRANGED FOR HORN AND PIANO

BY **MASON JONES**

ISBN 0-7935-5427-6

G. SCHIRMER, *Inc.*

DISTRIBUTED BY

7777 W. BLUEMOUND RD. P.O. BOX 13819 MILWAUKEE, WI 53213

FOREWORD

Much care has been taken in selecting material for FIRST SOLOS FOR THE HORN PLAYER. We feel that the sensibilities of the young student should be nourished from the beginning on the finest music available to him.

The range of each selection is well within the capabilities of a young performer, and no composition is of too long a duration. Such musical judgments as tempos and phrasing can be made with the advice of a teacher.

The "Brazilian Set" is intended to give enjoyment to the performer, and the Bellini aria from *Romeo and Juliet* will give him a chance to play recitatives. In fact each composition selected for this album will give the player an opportunity to learn how to express himself musically and how to solve musical problems that require a moderate technical acumen.

M. J.

CONTENTS

FIRST SOLOS FOR THE HORN PLAYER

Transcribed and Arranged by Mason Jones

1. Folksong Suite
The Ash Grove

*The Horn part has been transposed in the Piano part, the part itself is written in F.

Ye Belles and Ye Flirts

The Dusky Night

2. No More, I Have Heard Everything
(Non Più Tutto Ascoltai)

from: Scene with Rondo for Soprano and Orchestra, K. 490

Wolfgang Amadeus Mozart (1756 - 1791)

3. Horn Quintet

(Second Movement)

from: Quintet in E♭ for Horn, Violin, Two Violas and Cello, K. 407

Wolfgang Amadeus Mozart (1756-1791)

4. Air From Rosamunde

Franz Schubert (1797-1828)

5. The Picture of a Rose
(Das Bild der Rose)

Johann Friedrich Reichardt (1752-1814)

6. A Favorite Place
(Lieblingsplätzchen)

Felix Mendelssohn (1809 - 1847)

7. Love Song
(Minnelied)

Felix Mendelssohn

8. Andante Espressivo

from: Piano Sonata, Op. 109

Ludwig van Beethoven (1770-1827)

9. Marmotte

from No. 7 of Eight Songs, Op. 52

Ludwig van Beethoven

10. Farewell Song to Vienna's Citizens at the Departure of the Viennese Volunteers

(Abschiedsgesang an Wiens Bürger beim Auszug der Wiener Freiwilligen)

Ludwig van Beethoven

11. The Heavens Are Telling
(Die Ehre Gottes aus der Natur)
No. 4 of Six Sacred Songs by Gellert, Op. 48

Ludwig van Beethoven

22

12. Ich Liebe Dich
(I Love You)

Ludwig van Beethoven

24

13. German Dance

Ludwig van Beethoven

* Piano octavo higher

FIRST SOLOS

FOR THE

HORN
PLAYER

TRANSCRIBED AND ARRANGED FOR HORN AND PIANO

BY **MASON JONES**

ISBN 0-7935-5427-6

G. SCHIRMER, Inc.

DISTRIBUTED BY

HAL•LEONARD®
CORPORATION

7777 W. BLUEMOUND RD. P.O. BOX 13819 MILWAUKEE, WI 53213

CONTENTS

Piano   Horn

1

FIRST SOLOS FOR THE HORN PLAYER

Transcribed and Arranged by Mason Jones

Horn in F

1. Folksong Suite
The Ash Grove

Ye Belles and Ye Flirts

The Dusky Night

2. No More, I Have Heard Everything
(Non Più, Tutto Ascoltai)

Wolfgang Amadeus Mozart (1756-1791)

3. Horn Quintet, K. 407

(Second Movement)

Wolfgang Amadeus Mozart

4. Air From Rosamunde

Franz Schubert (1797-1828)

5. The Picture of a Rose
(Das Bild der Rose)

Johann Friedrich Reichardt (1752-1814)

hand stopped
open fingering on F Horn

6

6. A Favorite Place
(Lieblingsplätzchen)

Felix Mendelssohn (1809-1847)

7. Love Song
(Minnelied)

Felix Mendelssohn

8. Andante Espressivo
from: Piano Sonata, Op. 109

Ludwig van Beethoven (1770-1827)

9. Marmotte

Ludwig van Beethoven

10. Farewell Song to Vienna's Citizens at the Departure of the Viennese Volunteers
(Abschiedsgesang an Wiens Bürger beim Auszug der Wiener Freiwilligen)

Ludwig van Beethoven

8

11. The Heavens are Declaring
(Die Ehre Gottes aus der Natur)

Ludwig van Beethoven

12. Ich Liebe Dich
(I Love You)

Ludwig van Beethoven

13. German Dance

Ludwig van Beethoven

14. Theme and March

from: Choral Fantasia, Op. 80

Ludwig van Beethoven

15. Brazilian Set
Choros

Louis Gordon

Samba

16. Sweet Reverie

Peter Ilyich Tchaikowsky (1840-1893)

17. Song of April

Georges Bizet (1838-1875)

18. I hear as in a dream
(Je crois entendre encore)

Georges Bizet

19. Romance

Alexander Scriabin (1872-1915)

20. Misty, Silvery Moon
(Vaga Luna Che Inargenti)

Vincenzo Bellini (1801-1835)

21. Juliet's Song
(From Romeo and Juliet)

Recitativo e Romanza Gillietta
from: I Montecchi e Capuletti

Vincenzo Bellini

22. The Song of Khivria

Modeste Mussorgsky (1839-1881)

23. Bessie Bobtail

Samuel Barber

24. Song

Edward MacDowell (1861-1908)

14. Theme and March

from: Choral Fantasia, Op. 80

Ludwig van Beethoven

15. Brazilian Set
Choros

Louis Gordon

Samba

16. Sweet Reverie

Peter Ilyich Tchaikowsky (1840-1893)

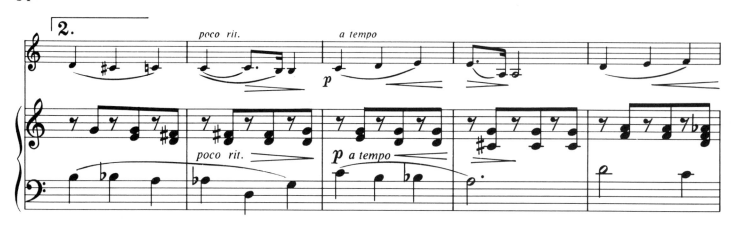

17. Song of April

Georges Bizet (1838 - 1875)

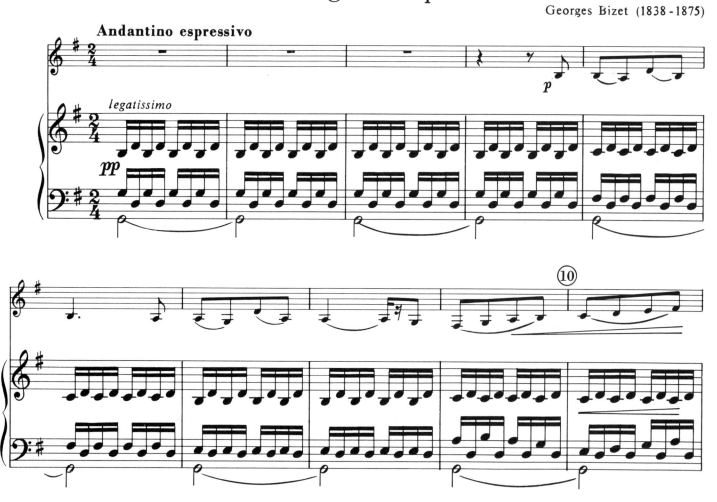

18. I hear as in a dream
(Je crois entendre encore)

from: The Pearl Fishers

Georges Bizet

19. Romance

Alexander Scriabin (1872-1915)

20. Misty, Silvery Moon
(Vaga Luna Che Inargenti)
from: Composizioni da Camera

Vincenzo Bellini (1801-1835)

21. Juliet's Song
(From Romeo and Juliet)

Recitativo e Romanza Gillietta
from: I Montecchi e Capuletti

Vincenzo Bellini

22. The Song of Khivria

Modeste Mussorgsky (1839-1881)

23. Bessie Bobtail

Samuel Barber

24. Song

from: Sea Pieces, Op. 55

Edward MacDowell (1861-1908)

G. SCHIRMER

DISTRIBUTED BY

HAL•LEON